CONTENT

G000153728

PICTURE CREDITS

The author is grateful to Goodwood Racecourse Ltd for the picture of the March and Sussex stands; to Wendy Meadway for The Moment of Suspension; to Anthony Reynolds for the Derby Bank at Hickstead; to Ginny Beard for the hunting pictures and to Bob Clother for pictures of polo.

INTRODUCTION

STATISTICS suggest there are at least 500,000 members of the genus *Equus caballus* in the south east. They come in all shapes and sizes, from children's ponies to top class race horses.

Every spare bit of grassland appears to be used for either ponies or horses and farmers gladly use their set-aside land for the livery of these animals. This is not always a good thing as half these private owners know so little about the animals in their charge one is shocked by their ignorance.

Riding schools are here to put them right but once some people have had a dozen or so lessons all too often they will buy a horse or pony and take their lives in their hands. For a horse, like any herd animal, can behave quite differently when taken away from its companions – bucking, shying and possibly bolting once turned in the direction of home.

Parents often say, when talking about the ability of their children: 'Oh yes, they are good riders – they have their own horses'. When riding schools instructors take these 'good riders' on a lesson it soon becomes obvious that they do not know the walk is a four time pace, the trot a two time and the canter, three.

A story with an object lesson concerns two children who were bought ponies for Christmas. Let us call the ponies Bill and Ben.

On their first day the children took them along a busy minor road and met a delivery lorry coming one way and a tractor the other. Bill swung round taking the girl back the way she had come and Ben cantered, with her brother, in the opposite direction. The ponies were not happy at finding themselves separated and Bill bucked and the girl was unseated. The boy stayed on and both ponies galloped back to their field. The lorry skidded into the back of the tractor, and the bedraggled children had to be rescued and taken home.

After that things did not improve and the children could only ride their ponies in the field or when an experienced rider rode along with them.

SUSSEX HORSE STORIES

Kenneth Quicke

S.B. Publications

By the same author:
Immortal Henry, the life story of a Lipizzaner stallion (Elek)
Let's Look at Horses, an illustrated guide to horse breeds
round the world (Wayland)

First published in 1996 by S. B. Publications
c/o 19 Grove Road, Seaford, East Sussex BN25 1TP

ISBN 1 85770 111 9

Typeset by CGB Lewes
Printed by Island Press Ltd. (01323) 490222 UK.

1 SHOW JUMPING

TWO young girls learned to ride at their local riding schools. One eventually chose the showing world as a career and the other show jumping. There is more to both these sports than the average person imagines and the story of the one who took up show jumping is certainly worth telling.

The Pony Club was a great help to her. It gave her encouragement and the chance to gain experience, as every weekend she was able to take part in competitions. Her parents were a considerable help to their daughter in her chosen career. One only has to look at the great names in the past to realise how essential is parental help – Ann Moore depended on her father as did Alan Oliver on his – but the Italian, d'Inzeo, had undoubtedly the most supportive of all parents.

One must remember and accept that Italy is the home of modern show jumping. It was the Italians who ended the long era of riding over fences leaning backwards in the saddle and with long stirrups. The change was brought about by a cavalry officer, Caprilli, at the end of

The young rider at one of her first jumping competitions in the 1950s.

the nineteenth century. At first there was surprise and hostility when he taught his students to lean forward over fences but his theory proved correct and the forward seat was officially adopted.

Our young girl's parents bought her her first pony and eventually she earned enough money to buy a better one. It was the turning point in her career. The pony went to the top at all local events and in the end to success at Hickstead. She has continued show jumping into adult life and has had a great many successes.

A good free-moving but obedient animal is essential to success but sometimes a show jumper is made by a clever rider. Every horse and every rider approaches the sport differently and it is only when the idiosyncrasies of both come together that there is magic in the result

This was proved when another girl rode the pony and lost in a competition in which he had always won in combination with his usual rider.

The art of show jumping is to choose the right approach and allow for all direction changes. One must remember that the horse's eyes are on the side of the head – probably for his protection when being pursued – and therefore he must be made aware of the next jump long before his final approach.

All these things have to be learnt at an early stage and if both horse and rider are instructed together the result can be a winner.

A show jumping course is walked by the rider first and the clever competitor can remember and judge the strides needed for that course and incidentally for his particular horse. He must allow for changes of direction and when to square the animal up for the final approach.

Some horses can be shortened in stride or lengthened by a clever rider. The more scientific the decisions, and the more the understanding how an individual animal will react to certain jumps, the better.

Sometimes 'against the clock' is difficult unless there is sufficient unity between both rider and horse. On some horses it is possible to change an approach at the last moment and still get a clear. This is achieved by a lot of shared understanding – and a lot of practice.

Many years ago, a local rider bought a young Irish mare that had all the ingredients for making a successful show jumper. After nearly two years of instruction and occasional wins at minor events she went to a

A winning combination in action

big show and things really happened.

The course was higher, but by not more than six inches, and contained a wall patterned with red and white squares. As the horse is believed to be wholly or partially colour blind this may have looked black and white to the mare but she suddenly behaved as if the wall was about to attack her. She shied repeatedly away from it even although she had jumped a similar one on previous occasions. The rider finally took a tumble and landed somewhere on the wall but the mare continued over several other jumps before being caught.

It was from that day the animal started improving as a professional jumper. It was as if she had needed the experience of that wall, or maybe the fright and feeling of insecurity given her by losing her rider was the turning point. This mare had always felt a secure rider in control on her back and it is possible that the experience of suddenly feeling weight and the control being dislodged created panic.

The mare went on to achieve great success. Her confidence was soon restored after practice over different wall jumps painted in squares, stars and zigzags. The rider, on the other hand, has suffered from recurring back trouble ever since.

Hickstead

DOUGLAS BUNN opened his All England Jumping Course at Hickstead in Sussex as long ago as 1960. The world of show jumping laughed and at first there was very little enthusiasm for this first attempt to provide a top class, purpose-built and permanent show jumping course.

Hickstead offered a challenge which could never be found in the best of Britain's county shows. Douglas Bunn was offering the riders the chance to gain the experience they needed of the sort of fences they were likely to encounter at European shows

Standards have risen and Hickstead played and continues to play a very important part in keeping Britain at the top of the international scene. It caters for not only the leading jumping riders but also for Pony Club members, Driving Derby competitors, dressage riders, and meetings of showing classes.

The club terrace and private boxes gives everything an air of elegance. The Prince of Wales' Cup, like a lot of the major international events, used to be held amid the Edwardian grandeur of Olympia. It came for the first time to Hickstead in 1971.

Douglas Bunn lives in the Manor House and the Master of Hickstead is constantly making new developments on the green acres of his parkland. He spent his boyhood on his father's Selsey farm on the lushness of the Sussex coastal plain. It was there he started riding and going to all the local shows. At the start of the Second World War the army took away forty of his father's horses but out of kindness they left two of the best jumpers behind.

Douglas realised that a bolder horse and fixed jumps was fast becoming necessary and changes were needed in the lay out of courses. There was disagreement at first but the problems were thrashed out and top riders supported Douglas Bunn's idea. He contended that related fences, although important, were just part of the technicalities of course building.

It is strange that the first permanent jumping course in Great Britain, which has had such an impact on show jumping, was first conquered by a West Country man, Tom Brake – and he rode his horse like he had

The Derby Bank at Hickstead. Photo by: Anthony Reynolds. LBIPP. LMPA.

done many times as a youngster across country.

The story told by Douglas Bunn concerns his journey to Hamburg, complete with pencil and paper to measure the Hamburg Jumping Derby's jumps. Despite thick snow he took a train to this course in Flottbeck to measure and record all the heights and distances and especially the dimensions of their Derby Bank. When he returned home he made the Hickstead bank one foot higher.

These permanent jumps had names like Devil's Dyke, Cornishman, Irish Bank, Road Jump and Derby Bank – all to become the famous names in competition.

From 1970 up to today the Derby Bank has maintained a height of 10ft 6inches and a spread at the base of 5ft 3inches. To include such an obstacle in British Show Jumping was an important event. Over the years the main ring has been joined by many more, all equipped with first class jumps to suit all grades of competition.

Hickstead can stable more than a thousand horses and most of the competitors come in their own mobile homes. The British Show Jumping Association recognised the value of the Hickstead pattern for in the first year out of seventy young riders' classes no less than fifty were held at Hickstead – the remainder at the Horse of the Year Show.

Nothing has changed the character of Hickstead. The beautiful backdrop of lawns and the avenue of ancient oak trees leading up to the house are still vistas of delight.

The International Horse Show is now at Hickstead, which proves the point that this show ground has everything to offer. The Burghley Horse trials are also held there and, of course, the Hickstead Jumping Derby is world famous.

Why is it that the classic contests originally started by Douglas Bunn more than thirty years ago are still such a success? The answer is that he has made the sport the best in its field with superb and skillful riders jumping courses that offer a real challenge.

Long may this continue.

2 SHOW PONIES.

THE girl who took up showing ponies had a different story. The showing world is a cut-throat one where money can help win the top prizes. It is judged on quality and that means good looks and performance.

This young girl was fortunate in having wealthy parents who could afford to buy from the best stud farms, places where each animal is bred with established quality from winning stock.

Of course she had to learn to adapt to her first pony, which was highly strung from a well-known but difficult line. And here is the good news. After tears and tantrums she mastered the little horse so well that she actually started winning in local shows.

A lot depends on how both horse and rider behave on the day – the girl was showing ability and understanding and the pony answering her well.

Young riders showing style and promise in their first showing class.

In all showing classes the animals must have balanced and correct

11

paces. The walk must be straight and true, the trot must throw the toe 'beyond the nose' in extension, and the canter be correct and flowing with the hocks creating the energy and rhythm.

Both girls ultimately succeeded in their different fields but it was the way in which they worked towards final countrywide acclaim that is important. The show jumper had to be successful to increase the value of her horses so that other aspiring show jumpers would come and buy them. With the proceeds she was able to buy top class animals to bring on.

The other young horsewoman, instead of going from Show Ponies to Show Hacks once she was out of the pony classes, started to present other people's ponies for them. Her knowledge and experience made her one of the best presenters in the country. So much so that for many years ponies, and the young riders trained by her, won the accolade of Pony of the Year.

All showing is very competitive. An owner of a beautiful Arab stallion could never ride him well enough to win in good company until one day circumstances changed. The class was too large to be judged in the small pre-judging ring so all the stallions were allowed in the Main Ring.

The atmosphere was electric – a large, noisy crowd, Strauss waltzes from the public address system. . . The animals went crazy and the beautiful stallion, quite regardless of the efforts of his owner, won the class hands down with extreme, never-to-be-forgotten movement and cadence.

On the right of this picture a lone rider – could it be an apparition of Darkie and his original owner?

3 A GHOST STORY
(with pictures)

THIS story, which has been handed round the stable yards for many years, is one that should interest those who still believe in ghosts.

A favourite hunter belonging to an old man had to be put down. His name was Darkie and he had lived a long life, surviving many illnesses and accidents.

The vets agreed that his condition was getting worse and when he started coughing and a cold turned to emphysema they thought it kinder to end his misery. But the old horse had a temporary recovery and was able to be ridden in light exercise. He did not take kindly to this and whenever he had the chance he would gallop off, which not only affected his lungs but also his arthritic joints. He had loved hunting all his life and had the spirit of a king. His owner loved him very much and on the night before the vets were due to put him down a strange thing happened.

Darkie was turned out in a paddock bordering a thick forest and when the groom went to fetch him in the evening he was nowhere to be seen. His owner and his neighbours searched everywhere in the fading light but despite secure paddock fences he had disap peared. The forest had encroached in parts of the land and because of the dense coppice and brambles the searchers had difficulty exploring all the paths. Finally they decided to leave the old horse out in the paddock for the night and a pile of hay and a trough full of water was provided for him.

The paddock gate had a horse-proof bolt but the next morning, when the groom came to open the stable, the old horse was contentedly standing in his box. The paddock gate was still firmly bolted.

The mystery of how he got out was never solved but finding him safe and contented was reward enough. However, his condition worsened that day and by evening the vets said it was unkind to keep him alive. His old owner insisted he had another night so it was arranged for the vets to come first thing in the morning.

That night Darkie disappeared from his stable and by morning he was back in his favourite paddock lying down, unable to get to his feet. The paddock gate was firmly shut. The vets arrived and at noon Darkie was painlessly put down, the mystery of the gate being dismissed as a prank by some local lads.

The body was taken away by a reputable knackerman and a wreath of summer flowers hung on the stable door. It was a sad day. Darkie had been around for so long and his old owner decided he would not buy another horse as he felt he was getting too old himself for galloping about the countryside.

The paddock became part of a bridleway and the local pony and riding clubs used the tracks nearly every day. Time passed and Darkie was forgotten by the locals until it came to light that many riders had seen a lone horse and rider in that part of the forest.

The old man and his grandchildren often walked in the forest and one day they saw the lone rider themselves. It was undoubtedly the spitting image of the old horse, but no amount of inquiries could reveal who the rider was or where they had come from.

Soon after another strange thing happened. The paddock gate, which was now never unbolted, was found open and as well as hoofprints, a cast shoe found on the ground.

This proved nothing until one summer day – an anniversary of the old horse's death, as it happens – some riders were going through that part of the forest and a friend pho-tographed them.

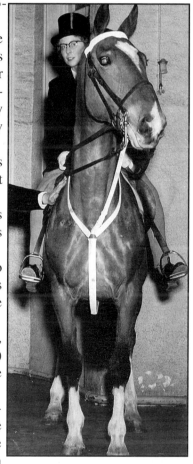

When the film was developed, sure enough, the lone rider on Darkie was there in the undergrowth. His old owner recognised the horse and he remem-bered that when he bought him many years previously he had been ridden by a girl wearing a light grey hat.

As the picture at the beginning of this chapter shows the lone rider on the right is quite clearly wearing just such a hat.

There was also a ghost that proved its presence on cine film on a cold winter's day in the hunting field.

Apparently this one was supposed to be the ghost of a famous huntsman's wife on her distinctive light bay mare called Plain Jane.

The horse had appeared at hunt balls, (as can be seen in the picture, right,) when she carried the huntsman's wife into the dance hall.

The lady in question died in a hunt-ing accident on her beloved Plain Jane and after the mare's death they were often seen, and once filmed, riding with hounds across that same hilly bit of land where the fatality occurred.

4 REST HOMES FOR HORSES

THERE are quite a few rest homes for horses in the south and most have good intentions. However it is not always kind to retire a favourite horse or pony by putting him out to grass. He must have attention every day to survive.

On soft going he would not wear his feet down, so the regular inspection from a qualified blacksmith is a must. Also, if he is native bred, lush grazing could be a cause of lameness in the form of laminitis or cracked heel.

The owner of a very beautiful Lippizaner stallion retired his horse to a rest home run by a charity. On the face of it the place was very suitable. It was an old stud farm with double-fenced fields and large airy boxes. The little stallion loved the freedom of fields, after many years doing High School in a large indoor school, He was a famous horse, having completed a long ride with the rider wearing full battle armour and had been ridden in many films by some top actors.

Sadly one day he was galloping about and fell into a ditch and was caught between fences so badly that he died of his injuries before a vet could get to him.

The 'retirement thought' was a misguided one for this particular animal, as it can be for many others.

An owner of a well known riding school suggested to one of these charities that he could give a good home to some of their 'retired' horses only to be told in no uncertain terms that they always sent re-homed animals to private stables, NEVER to riding schools.

The owner laughed at this for every horse he owned in his riding school had come from private stables. He felt he was 'rescuing' them because some of the private homes were so awful.

One beautiful Connemara had been ridden so badly that the owner could not get him to leave his stable yard. Another had taken to rearing from the pain of an inappropriate bit; one had bolted back to his stable every time he was taken out; others had been lamed by bad shoeing or ignorant jumping routines – the list was endless.

An old horse belonging to a very experienced horseman went blind over three years and nothing could be done for him. During all that time the owner rode him, acting as his eyes but the time came when the kindest thing was to have him painlessly put down, and that is what he did.

This horse had a wonderful life with lovely fields to enjoy in freedom and a rider who kept him balanced in all paces. Many people were shocked and said he should have been retired. Can you imagine how awful that would have been for him?

A group of horses rescued from a poor retirement home.

5 RACE HORSES

DOWNLAND is excellent for the training and exercise of race horses, which is why Sussex has so many racing stables. Early morning warm-ups and exercise gallops, to bring the animals into condition, are sights worth seeing. There are training tracks for this purpose with a special surface to protect the horses' legs. A light tarmac all-weather surface is also available but it is not always suitable for fast work.

Racing gallops come later when the muscles are hardened and the lungs are stronger. Many a race horse has dropped out with either a bro-ken leg or a heart-attack – it is only the best that can go on and win. Winning is the name of the game and trainers know when they have a winner after only a few months. Studs breed from this stock and top stables are sought out by the wealthy potential race horse owners.

The gallop is a pace of four time, unlike the canter which is three. This fast pace is difficult to sit to and the jockeys learn to ride with short stirrups, virtually standing in the saddle. It needs good balance, 'giving' hands and knowing how to use a stick but it is amazing how many so-called jockeys have not been taught the real basics of equi-tation.

A number of good trainers today believe this should be remedied and they have their jockeys taught to ride before letting them ride exercise on the thoroughbreds. However, this does not stop owners allowing their friends to ride exercise – and some of them are useless in the sad-dle. It is not a wise thing to do as the amateur on a fresh horse only needs a buck or an unprepared gallop to make him take a tumble.

The evolution of the thoroughbred is interesting. The accepted ances-tor, who was barely larger than a fox, possessed four metacarpal bones on the forefoot, and three digits, or metatarsal bones on the hind-feet. Its teeth too were adapted for eating the undergrowth of the forests which it inhabited.

The modern horse is a descendant of the genus *Equus*, the three toed hipparion. During evolution and change in surroundings, the extinct horse developed longer and stronger middle digits and side digits disappeared altogether. Dentition also changed. As it left the forest for open prairie the animal grew molar teeth for grazing, chopping the vegetation with the incisors and masticating with the molars.

English equine blood was improved by the introduction of Norman strains. It is said that horse racing is the Sport of Kings and certainly it was King Henry II who imported sires into England from the Continent for the first time in an attempt to improve the strain.

Henry VIII and Queen Elizabeth both kept race horses, which were bred at Middle Park. It is from this stable that the well-known six furlong race for two-year-olds gets its name.

A notable point in the history of the thoroughbred was the arrival of the Darley Arabian in the year 1705 but it was not until 1728 that an illustrious stallion, the Godolphin Arab – or Barb because he came from the Barbary Coast – arrived to fulfil a large part in the equine eugenics of the Stud Book.

During the last fifty years more than sixty per cent of Grand National winners have been bred in Ireland and it is considered that the climate and pasture there is superior to that of England.

In 1689 a famous horse known as the Byerley Turk went over to Ireland with King William's army and became one of the most important sires and a pillar of the Stud Book.

When he retired, a six year old who won many races in 1884, including the Derby, appeared on the stage at Drury Lane in a racing scene from *The Prodigal Daughter.* In the making of the film *March Hare* one of the film jockeys was told by the director to make sure his horse was lying third in the race as they passed in front of the camera. This he succeeded in doing but he could not stop the animal until had completed three circuits of the course.

People often take shares in a race horse and it gives them added pleasure to go and see 'their horse' in a race. Even getting placed is exciting and as for winning – it is very much a bonus.

A number of race horses get discarded when their form is not good as owners find it is not economical to keep unproven stock. Often these animals are sold as hacks. Their pedigree is a good selling point and

Two ex-race horses now used as hacks.

keeps the price high, for even a losing race horse has a quality pedigree and the hacking fraternity like telling their friends they have a thoroughbred even if he is slow in the gallop, pigeon-toed in front and cow-hocked behind.

The thoroughbred has a reputation for comfort, easy stride and clean transitions. This is not always true because often its trot has a high throwing action which an amateur finds uncomfortable and when he gets excited he can bolt unless reschooled as a hack.

Glorious Goodwood is the most scenically beautiful of all race courses, set as it is on the South Downs 700 ft above sea level.

Racing was introduced there by the third Duke of Richmond to oblige the officers of the Sussex regiment of which he was Colonel. For years the Earl of Egremont had held races for them at Petworth Park but when he ceased to do so the Duke of Richmond had a course built on his estate at Goodwood.

That was in 1801. The first meeting took place in April 1802 but this was altered to July in the following year. The military duties of the founder of Glorious Goodwood prevented him spending any length of

The March and Sussex stands at Goodwood.

time in England and it was in 1812, while he was serving with his regiment overseas, that the Goodwood Cup was run for the first time – and won by a horse named Shoestring from four others.

The fifth duke developed a keen interest in racing after wounds incurred at the Battle of Orthez in the Peninsula War and an accident when riding to hounds forced him to give up hunting. He filled the Goodwood stables, designed by Sir William Chambers, with race horses and even introduced a new method of starting races – by waving a flag rather than just shouting GO.

The post war popularity of racing at Goodwood has led to the introduction of additional fixtures. A May meeting was introduced in 1968 and the July meeting extended for five more days. A motor racing circuit, a golf course and an airfield were built in the sixty acre park

The old stand was demolished in 1979 and was replaced by the March stand which won the annual Concrete Society Award and was opened by Queen Elizabeth pulling a rug off a bronze horse sculpted by Dame Elizabeth Frink.

In 1989 the new Charlton stand was opened and in 1990 the Sussex Stand which won a commendation from the Royal Fine Arts Commission. In 1995 the first Sunday meeting was held, bringing the total number of race days at Goodwood to nineteen.

6 THE BLACKSMITH

THE blacksmith got his name from the black smoke made by his coal fires when working iron into horseshoes. Today he is known as a farrier and must pass examinations before practising the art of shoeing.

In the nineteenth century it was one of the most important jobs because all transport depended on the horse. Owners would have to drive or ride to the smithy whereas nowadays the farrier will come to them. Some will still shoe hot but these days it is more practical to shoe cold. It is accepted that the fit can be a degree or so better when the shoe is hot because it makes the horn mould itself more closely to the shoe.

Shoes of all types.

Today the iron comes ready in form and size and the farrier will hammer it into shape if and when he finds it necessary, whereas the old blacksmiths had to make every shoe an exact fit.

Farriers admit that nailing shoes onto horses' feet is a necessary evil, but nothing has been invented yet to replace it. No glue is adequate, due to the expansion of the foot on contact with the ground. It is as a result of this contact that nails loosen and shoes work thin.

For medical purposes there is a shoe called an Easi-boot but it cannot be ridden in successfully – those who have tried very soon find that the shoes are flying off in all directions. It does, however, serve a useful purpose as does gluing light shoes onto young stock out at grass.

Racehorses have very light shoes made from alloy of aluminium and they are replaced after every race.

Because horses' feet grow, rather like one's finger nails, the shoes have to be checked every four to six weeks. Some horses grow a lot of foot and the horn can overlap the shoe. A worn shoe can cause a risen clench which indicates the nails have loosened.

In hot climates, if the work is mostly on unmetalled tracks and the horn of the hoof is hard and dry, it is possible to work horses without shoes, but usually it is safer only to leave the hind shoes off. When they are worked unshod great care must be taken, and the hoof wall slightly rounded off to prevent any splitting of the horn.

Your farrier will know the meaning of the following words which relate to the horse's foot:

Coffin, navicular, coronet, pedal, pastern, perforatus, extensor, white line, horn, frog, ligament, tendon, hoof wall, sole, bars, heel, cartilage, mule, boxy, club, pottery.

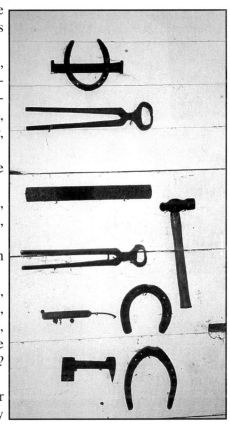

And then words describing the shoes:

Web, cover, branch, seating, saucer, fuller, calkin, concave, clips, featheredge.

And the tools, some of which are pictured right:

Hammer, buffer, drawing, searcher, ragstone, rasp, apron, pincers, turning hammer, tongs, pritchel, heel cutter, anvil, slice and poker – shall we go on? Phew!

So you will also know their meaning here is an explanatory list – starting with:

THE FOOT.

Coffin, navicular, pedal and pastern are all bones in the foot.

Coronet is the top of the foot – the coronary band.

Perforatus and extensor are tendons.

White line is the line inside the hoof wall.

Horn is the substance of the foot.

Frog is the triangular shape on the treading surface.

Wall, sole, bars – side, treading surface and sides of hoof.

Mule, boxy, club – shape of the foot.

Pottery – action of the feet.

THE SHOES

Web, cover, branch, seating are all parts of the shoe.

Saucer, fuller, calkin, concave, clips – groove for the nails and extra metal bits to help action.

THE TOOLS

Hammer, buffer, drawing, searcher – used for paring and removing old shoes.

Ragstone, rasp, pincers, tongs, pritchel are used in hot shoeing.

Heel cutter is for preparing the shoe.

Apron, anvil, slice and poker – used for work at the forge.

7 HUNTING

In full cry

HUNTING has been going on for centuries and has been accepted by farmers and country people – the farmers in the hope it will stop foxes from killing lambs, hens and small stock and those taking part for an exciting gallop across country.

On a cold winter's day when horses are fresh and ridden in mixed company, they are often difficult to handle. It is this that gives hunting the thrill that is missing in other equestrian sports. Horses revert back to their herd instincts and can get over excited so that the riders need knowledge and experience to hold them.

Farmers often build hunt jumps, consisting of parallel bars sloping inwards from the base to one top bar, in field fences and install weighted hunt gates which will close automatically when horses and riders have gone through.

The Master huntsman and whipper-in control the hounds and the field and although there are many opportunities for the chase, on some days there is a lot of waiting about at covert while the huntsman casts the hounds in a wood or spinney likely to hold a fox.

It takes a great deal of skill and determination to stay all day and not even have one good run. Foxes are clever animals and one wonders whether it is only the old and infirm that are finally caught.

There will always be people who object to a sport in which an animal is hunted and killed, but it is a fact that non-hunting farmers have their foxes shot and in one season this can rid their fields of forty foxes whereas the hunt may kill only six.

The anti-hunting crowds think only of the foxes, seldom the horses. Often good quality thoroughbreds are ridden by heavyweights and it is common for injury to wind and limb to occur. Horses have to carry their own weight as well as that of the rider and galloping over rough terrain can cause them trouble.

One story about the introduction to hunting of two youngsters who owned Welsh Mountain ponies is enlightening.

The scene is a children's meet at the start of a season. Moving off was calm and without incident but as soon as the ponies sensed unknown company and new ground ahead they lost their usual quiet demeanour and became difficult to control.

At the first gallop the young riders were left behind – but only for a minute. The ponies took the bit and were off like lightning. One pony jumped through a small hedge and landed in a field of cows and the other pony dashed about trying to find him.

Someone opened a hunt gate and the pony and rider dashed through (without a thank you!). The cows started to panic and found the hole in the hedge so that the hunt was soon surrounded by a herd of good Sussex cattle. The field took a turn back through the village and the locals enjoyed the sight of the gentry mingling with the cows – but the farmer was livid.

By the time the ponies found each other again hounds were in full cry and their riders had no choice but to join in. As hunt jumps loomed up the children shut their eyes and clung on; they tried to get the ponies to leave the hunt and turn for home but the animals were so excited

The Crawley and Horsham Foxhounds and (below) the Southdown and Eridge Hunt. Photo by Ginni Beard.

they just carted them back again.

Finally one of the children parted company over a ditch and the other got caught up in a tree and was left hanging there, while the hunt disappeared over the horizon. Fortunately at that moment a young woman on a beautiful hunting pony came to the aid of the children and helped them catch their runaway ponies and guided them onto a lane which led to home. How much truth there is in this story it is difficult to imagine – something is added every time it is told.

Another story concerns an eighty year old woman who never missed a hunting season, always turning up immaculately dressed, riding sidesaddle on an elderly, much loved mare. She stayed all day and was always in at the kill.

On one wet windy day, when the going was rough, she jumped a ditch and her horse pecked badly on the other side. She was unseated and landed heavily on the opposite bank. Several followers stopped to help, and the horse, despite the excitement, returned and stood by her side. In fact it was the horse that helped her to her feet. The mare stood rock still just putting her head down as if offering her neck as a prop. With some help from the bystanders, the elderly rider remounted and went off after the hunt. It was a strenuous day but both she and her mare cheerfully hacked the three miles home afterwards – and eventually settled in for the night.

Neither appeared to be any the worse for the long day but when the staff arrived the next morning there was no sign of the mistress of the house and the stable door was still closed. Usually the mare had been fed and her owner was up and about, ready for another day.

It was discovered that neither of them had awakened that morning – both the elderly owner and her much loved mare had died peacefully in their sleep.

Her son commissioned a well known artist to do an oil painting of his mother looking decidedly elegant on her magnificent mare. In the background are horses and hounds and a lovely view of the Downs in winter.

8 DRIVING

IT does not seem all that time ago that horses were seen being driven along on the road, pulling carts containing everything from milk to fresh vegetables, and along every navigable river and canal bank heavy horses were towing barges packed with freight.

Now everything has changed. Deliveries are now done by mechanical transport and those rivers and canals that remain navigable are devoted to pleasure boating. Today driving has become another horsey sport with smart single turn-outs, tandem harness, pairs and fours-in-hand competing in various events.

Years ago all cobby Irish and Welsh horses were sold as ride-and-drive. It was presumed that their strong legs and good shoulders meant

Vera Cody driving her Palomino, Goldie, in competition.

they had been broken to drive, and as riding them came naturally, they could be ridden quite safely too. The type was true and anyone with a bit of knowledge could accept this as fact.

It was also thought that driving-cobs looked better hogged and docked, but animal lovers thought it was cruel to cut off manes and tails. If the driving horses were kept in stables this was not so, but if they were kept out at grass, where they needed their long hair for protection against flies, it was unkind.

The most sought after horses for driving are the hackneys for they are well bred and have the limbs for walking briskly with a spring to the step, and a trot which is lofty, smooth and progressive.

Most hackneys are descended from a brown stallion called Mathias, foaled in 1895, but after many centuries it became a horse for general riding as distinct from a warhorse. In 1883 a stud book was formed for English Trotting Horses. After the turn of this century these were in great demand as stylish high-stepping driving horses.

The modern hackney is from 14–3 to 15–2 hands high. There is also a hackney pony which has evolved from the horse during the past hundred years and is now accepted as a separate breed. It has extreme action in the trot, abounding energy and can be from 12 to 14 hands high.. Hackneys can be driven in single or double harness or in tandem – one behind the other.

The good old pony and trap, known as a family turn out, is still an attractive example of the past.

A local horseman had always believed cobby ponies were indeed ride-and-drive until one day he bought a bay, hogged and docked pony with a good shoulder and strong straight legs.

He was so certain this was a driver that he invited his wife and family and his neighbours to watch him putting the little fellow into harness and setting up the traces.

When it was ready, everyone admired the turn-out as the prettiest picture they had ever seen. They all stood back – and the unthinkable happened.

The little pony eyed them once before taking off like a Ferrari. Pony and dogcart, immaculate grooming and shiny paintwork, disappeared in a cloud of dust. It was no use chasing it and there seemed no chance of stopping it either. The owner was terribly embarrassed, especially when the neighbours thought it funny and started to laugh.

The pony took the nearest route through the yard gate, turned left onto the main road and carried on as if a lion were on his tail. The farce went on for nearly half an hour until he saw another pony in a field and turned sharply to say hello. The turn was his undoing as it took him into a narrow cul de sac where he was caught by the farmer..

One should never trust the term ride-and-drive without checking it out but many people still take the breeder's word that 'has been ridden' (and schooled?) means a youngster which is ready to go on.

Some young businessmen thought up a wonderful idea to make lots of money – how about buying four white horses and a gilded coach to hire out for weddings?

They acquired four white/grey mares from Holland and had an old coach painted up in shiny gold and white paint. Unfortunately, the first wedding couple to be driven from the church were so frightened they got out and walked. The business failed very soon afterwards.

In Sussex there are breeders of Shire horses which are still driven in weight pulling competitions and one recorded a weight of seventeen tons. They are descendants of the mediaeval Great Horse and in 1878 the Shire Horse Society was formed.

In the film *Gypsy and the Gentleman* there was a scene with a coach and four and the director asked if any of the stunt riders could drive. One spoke up and said he had driven horses many times but he was surprised to be faced with a coach and four when he had only ever driven a pony and trap. But he managed to drive it wearing a purple dress to double for the film's star, Melina Mercouri.

A scene in which he had to drive the coach over a bridge and into a lake was more difficult and had to be done in easy stages so as not to injure the horses. He had to position the coach so that it would appear to be hanging precariously over the parapet – without actually going over and taking the horses with it.

The hero and heroine were then thrown into the lake where the hero had to drown Melina Mercouri with what they described as the kiss of death. The actor was never keen on doing the shot himself so the poor old stunt rider did it for him.

9 HORSE AUCTIONS

HORSES sold at auction can create feelings of either sadness or joy. Sadness because often the animals are sold through neglect or poverty and joy when a beautiful young horse is sold to a good and knowledgeable home.

 The auctioneers reserve the right to refuse bidding by any one person and in case of a dispute between two or more approved bidders the animals will be put up again at the discretion of the auctioneer, who will be the sole arbitrator in any dispute.

One of the funniest things happened to two women who were bidding for the same horse – they kept on bidding until at one point the auctioneer found they were bidding against themselves, so exciting had they found the experience. No one else was in the bidding, so he had to go steadily from one to the other, until one got a good nudge from her husband and stopped waving her catalogue.

Private auctions can be distressing when a stud or riding school is sold after operating for many years. Horsemen and women are sentimental about animals they have known and handled in these cases. When the owner of one establishment retired it seemed the best thing to sell the stock at auction. The horses and ponies were not very young but it was hoped good homes could be found for them. A number of those who bid for their favourite animal did it out of affection, not with knowledge and forethought; they had no idea where they would keep the animal so in their haste the wrong homes were accepted.

A few went to local riding schools where they were worked too hard but others were bought by loving and experienced owners. These were the lucky ones and the stable owner, even after fifteen years of retirement, still receives news of these animals together with photographs of them – and Christmas cards.

Auctions at stud farms can be different because people know what they are doing and buy for selected breeding purposes, although one animal, which had ultimately to be dealt with by the RSPCA, was bought as a foal by a loving bidder and this poor little chap was found living in an old coalshed in a small backyard, fed on a tiny lawn with a bowl of rice crispies twice a day. The owners thought 'oats' meant anything from a breakfast packet.

One of the saddest auctions was when twenty little donkeys were sold after a disastrous season of donkey rides on a beach. Their condition had been condemned and a licence refused. Donkeys are sad little people at the best of times but at auction, with saddle sores and untrimmed feet, they were pathetic.

AT THE STABLES

Metro-Goldwyn-Mayer Studios   British Studios Ltd.

ELSTREE WAY, BOREHAM WOOD, HERTS

Catalogue of

IMPORTANT UNRESERVED SALE

of

20 High-class
HUNTERS AND HACKS

including some outstanding Horses of great promise
worth special attention

MAY BE INSPECTED ON MORNING OF SALE

Messrs.

HARLAND & SON

G. H. Pickard, M.B.E., T.D., F.R.I.C.S., F.A.I.   W. Harding Young, F.A.I.

When the films are in the can studios usually auction off the horses that have carried the stars and stunt riders.

33

10 HORSE DEALING

HORSE DEALING must be one of the oldest trades in the world. Even down here in good old Sussex horses seem to be bought and sold everywhere. A number of stables profess to be dealing in Irish horses, but a greater number have animals bought and sold, or exchanged, through auction or from private owners.

One late afternoon during the winter a couple of customers bought what they thought were a pair of spotted ponies for their twin daughters' birthday presents. The ponies arrived home in the dark and unloaded easily, were housed side by side in the stable yard and, after a feed, came to their stable doors where everyone admired the pretty little spotted heads – then settled them in for the night.

The following day the groom arrived early to start work and one of his first jobs was to clean out the boxes and give the new ponies a brisk grooming. Eventually the owners came out with their twin daughters, who were jumping about with enthusiasm, to make the formal presentation.

The groom presented the ponies, tidy and glossy of coat, but there was great concern when it was discovered that only one pony had spots – the other one had lost his spots overnight.

The groom said he had to wash off some black spots but they were quite clean otherwise. The dealer declared that he had never sold them as a matching pair of spotted ponies – just as good steady children's ponies – which they were. Fortunately the twins loved them dearly, spots or not, and the joke was shared among the dealing fraternity.

Dealers seen to appear at every sale, even private ones where prices can be too high for them, but it is a way of life. They are there, watching, listening and sharing jokes.

Despite what people think horse dealers are not such a dishonest bunch. The hardcore are as honest as a suspicious public will allow them to be. People will say they never sell to dealers but these same people will often buy from them.

One story that needs to be told, however, concerns a young horse from a bad home, where he was never fed properly and lived most of his life in a stable much too small. He developed a temper and would attack anyone who approached him. A dealer decided to send him out of the Sussex area and sent the horse to an auction in the north, making sure that his name was not mentioned in the sale particulars.

Six months later an amazing thing happened. The dealer had a letter from someone in Scotland. They said it had taken them a long time to trace him but they understood he had owned a young horse, and by their description – a light bay with distinctive white markings – it was undoubtedly the same one.

The dealer thought they were going to sue him for selling a horse with a dangerous disposition, but no, they merely wanted to ask him details of the previous homes and how he was bred. Apparently the little horse had gone straight into winning jumping competitions all over the country, his name had never been out of the winners. They adored the animal, he had never let them down, and the reason for tracing the dealer was to ask him if he could find them another one just as good.

A well known Sussex dealer sold a lovely Palomino to what appeared to be a good home, taking a yearling in part exchange. The yearling was healthy, with a vet's certificate of soundness, and had been bought from a reputable stud.

Unfortunately it had been given as a present to the Palomino customer with the assumption that it could be ridden straight away. The exchange was a successful one and the Palomino, being a five year old and schooled, much more suitable. The animal left the dealing yard rugged and bandaged, long white mane and tail spotless, golden coat glinting with health.

A year later the dealer was approached to buy back the Palomino as the family had lost interest in riding. He agreed to make an offer, but imagine his horror when arriving at the so called livery stable he found it just a jumble of old sheds in a muddy field.

The Palomino was standing on a pile of dirty sawdust with a small bowl of nuts and a tiny haynet looking out into a paddock which was a sea of mud with nothing growing except ragwort. It would not have taken the livery owner, with her six helpers, an hour to have pulled this up and burnt it. The Palomino was rubbed sore, very dirty and had wire cuts over his chest. The only water was in an old cracked bath.

There were many apologies and, after bartering for the original price, the owner accepted a fair one which the dealer felt obliged to offer, if for no other reason than to rescue this lovely animal from just a poor home.

At one time dealers tried to be first in the Horses for Sale column in a weekly paper by starting their advertisement with ab. One had pride of place for many years with A Bargain every Time until another dealer thought up a better one with Abandon your Search. In the end the editor changed the system by starting with the animals' size – little ones first.

11 LONG DISTANCE RIDING

LONG distance riding is a sport that has recently become fashionable, yet it must have be one of the oldest of all equestrian pursuits.

The fact that a horse could be used for transport and went further and faster that any man on foot has caused it to survive as it has. There are tales of long army marches, of the migration of tribes. Doctors used to ride out to patients in emergencies and messengers would ride over hostile land into battlefields.

The Arab horse features high in the placings for endurance rides, which could be due to their ability to cope with hot and humid climates.

In Sussex, as in many other parts of Britain, native ponies crossed with a thoroughbred or Arab are popular, although now Appaloosas, Trakehners, Quarter horses and Haflingers are showing the way.

Competitions are organised by various associations which have rules to safeguard the horses. There are many different lengths of ride but the top event is the hundred miles a day ride.

Britain has been involved in the sport seriously for the last fifty years. Competitive rides are over a set course within a certain time limit, and these are judged on the condition of the animal's pulse and respiration, evidence of tiredness, sweating or being tucked up.

Training is as serious as for any other sport. It involves lunging every day, hacking with time lengthened over a period of a week's work, sometimes fast work for up to an hour and the usual rest period of one whole day a week.

In the 1950s there were two long endurance rides by a stunt rider to advertise the film *Richard III*. Both rides were over 200 miles and, as the rider was wearing a full set of battle armour, both he and the horse needed periods of rest. The rides were therefore divided into thirty mile a day sections and the RSPCA helped by finding overnight accommodation for the participants.

The first of these rides was not checked by anyone but on the second

The author, in full armour, rode from Wolverhampton to London and London to Norwich on Black Bess to publicise the film Richard III.

there was someone following the horse and rider all the way to make sure the mileage was correct, and it was this ride that appeared in the *Guiness Book of Records* as the Longest Recorded Ride in Full Armour.

Here is the story of the rides – straight from the horse's mouth – told by Black Bess who completed both of them.

'
Perhaps it was because I am Irish my master chose me for the job. I've done some funny things in my seven years but this was the oddest of them all.

At first I thought it was another film job when a producer fellow suddenly shouts action and we have two minutes of utter chaos – followed by an hour of bliss munching grass or hay.

I suspected something was up when my mane and tail were washed and bandages put on my legs. Then the next day I was put into a trailer and kept there for hours travelling over country I had never seen before.

I spent a night in a large loose box and given so many oats I couldn't believe my eyes – then the next day another trailer journey but only half an hour long.

We arrived at a large building and I was taken into a yard with lots of people. I neighed but no horses answered. Then I was dressed in bright red and gold satin rugs, such odd things and they flapped round my legs. I told everyone my bridle should not have tickly feathers on it, but they would not listen.

I was led round a corner and a dreadful shining object, with more tickly feathers, clanked up to me. I shied away but then I heard a voice and realised it was my master, dressed up like me. He had to be helped into the saddle and then all the people started talking and taking photographs. The cameras were much smaller that the film cameras and no one screamed ACTION.

Every one cheered when we left the building and started up the road. Ah! I thought, at last we are going somewhere, I do hope it's grassy – but oh! dear, it was roads all the way. I had to pass noisy things and objects I had never seen before and people invited me into shops and gave me titbits.

On the first afternoon it was bewildering to be led into a kind of large hall with lots of things hanging on the walls. Afterwards I was led out by my master and taken to a stable for the night. I decided it could not be film work because the stables were different from the ones under canvas in the last film. What could it mean? As I had plenty of hay and bedding it didn't really seen to matter.

The next day was the same, all roads and cities, kind people and tit-bits. The day after we had a canter on some grass and stopped at a farm where I had a roll in a tiny paddock. My master was angry because I still had my saddle on, but it was heavy and the satin things irritating. The next day and the one after that was spent posing for the cameras – I wondered whether I was the Horse of the Year at last.

I was stabled at one place with lots of little ponies galloping about outside. I pushed at my door and the bolt came undone so I had a lovely chase with the ponies until someone caught me. My daily routine was becoming boring – another day, more cameras, more titbits – my master stopping to give a scroll of paper to men at town halls every day.

We were surrounded at one time with crowds of children – just think of the titbits. My master can be a rotten spoilsport, we only stayed there a few minutes, then off to another stable for the night.

On the last day the country started to disappear again. Oh dear, I thought, have I been tricked into going in a large circle and now I am back where I started? Roads, buses, cement mixers – ugh!

Then I had a wild thought. The buses looked familiar. I was approaching home again – not Ireland of course, not in my wildest dreams – but my own stable back in Sussex. Well, really, isn't that odd-est thing? Hours away in a trailer and my master makes me walk all the way home again.

I was feeling a bit upset about it and I not only refused to pose for those silly little cameras I went right off my oats as well. I still feel sore about the whole thing but I am HOME again and I can boss the ponies about in the paddock (they haven't a clue what a glamorous animal I really am), so I suppose I mustn't grumble.

When is the next film?'

Another long ride took place in the early seventies when a group of ten white/grey horses were ridden from London to their country home on the South Downs. The journey was done in two stages with an overnight stop at a stable in Ashdown Forest.

In those days the roads – even the A22 – had verges of some kind but the route was planned to use side roads whenever possible. The shoes were new on before they left London but one horse had risen clenches and a blacksmith had to be found on the way before the shoes were lost.

The organiser of the ride went ahead, in a Landrover with trailer, to scout for places to feed and water the horses. He carried a map with directions for services, including vets, and had a supply of waterproof clothing for the riders.

The horses, all mares, were going down to a Sussex farm to start a breeding programme. Two stallions, one Arab and the other Lippizaner, had been boxed down in readiness.

The venture was successful and all but two of the mares had healthy, lovely looking foals. They were born dark grey but, as white is the dominant colour, by the time they were four years old they all had grown strong white coats. One or two retained dappled quarters for another two years but after that even the dapples faded.

The white horses on their way from London to Sussex.

Competitors in fancy dress join in the fun of the sack race at a pony club camp.

12 GYMKHANA AND PONY CLUB

GYMKHANA is a word meaning a public display of athletics and sporting competition – especially horse riding. In India the army used the word for such occasions and even the game of polo derived from it.

Today the term gymkhana is used for children's horsey games and there are many of them, the most common being Musical Hats where competitors take a hat off a pole when the music stops.

One brilliant little 12–2 hands high pony enjoyed it so much that the rider did nothing, he did everything for her – except take the hat. He knew that when the music stopped he had to turn in and on one or two occasions he did this so suddenly and precisely that his rider lost balance and fall off.

His name was Bracken and although he specialised in Musical Hats he could beat all the other ponies at bending round poles without knocking them over and in the Handy Pony competition which involves bending, going through a gate and jumping a brush fence. The Bending Race is by elimination and the Handy Pony judged on the fastest time.

A good gymkhana pony is rare and must be accepted along with successful show and jumping horses. They are a delight to watch and all top competitors in the show ring are better for having gymkhana'd a good pony in their youth.

The Pony Club encourages competition in every branch of the sport and it guarantees the development of a rider's independent seat, sympathetic hands and strong legs.

For many years Margaret Sheffield ran the Southdown Pony Club but ten years ago it became so big that it was divided into three – Southdown, East Sussex and West Sussex.

At one time there were eighty teams from the pony clubs entered for polo at Cowdray Park and the group from Southdown were trained for a time by Bob Clother, who played polo for eighteen years in Nigeria.

Polo in the Pony Club is comparatively new but is having great success. In fact a large number of this country's top adult players have come up from this beginning.

Members of pony clubs usually have their own ponies although some clubs hire from reputable schools in their area. One of the most exciting things is to go to one of the club camps during summer holidays. They are well organised, sometimes under canvas, and at suitable places where the ponies can be living ideally in livery or out at grass. The New Forest is a favourite spot and the riding facilities there excellent – as they are in such areas as Ashdown Forest, where the going is good across country and the bridleways kept in good condition.

Polo at Cowdray and (below) the polo team from the Southdown Pony Club.

13 POLO

INDEPENDENT seat, sympathetic hands, strong legs – how important are these for the polo player. The sport came to England more than a hundred years ago from India where it was played by army officers who discovered this ancient game while stationed there.

At first the ponies were native to each country in which the game was played. Chinese ponies were used in Hong Kong, Arabians in Egypt. Eventually the Australian ponies asserted their superiority and were always been recognised in the top games.

A special type of small horse was bred in Sussex – a blood hunter type, standing at 15 hands. With the stud book founded on native ponies and small thoroughbreds, the limiting height was 14–2 but this was abandoned in the early 1920s.

Players did finally put size and pacing before any other consideration and it was decided that the best height was about 15–2 hh, which would give the polo pony enough substance for the job. Judging by the weights imposed on the backs of these athletic horses it was a necessary change.

The requisites for a good polo pony are not unlike those for the gymkhana pony – speed, stamina, balance, courage; and a temperament neither lazy nor over excitable.

By the time polo started again after the Second World War it was the Argentine ponies that became the main source of supply and nowadays only mares that have proved themselves in the sport are put to stud.

It is an exciting game to watch, very fast and skilful. The riders have to be extremely clever in the use of the polo stick and handling the horses in turns and twists all from the hock and a short, sharp gallop.

A chukker, which is a period of play, is quick and strenuous and, like good gymkhana ponies, these well bred little animals are quick to learn the signals until their responses become automatic.

One local boy, who thought he knew all the answers, borrowed a very well schooled pony for his first chukker but the animal had been trained by a clever and experienced horseman, obeying his every move.

The new rider had not perfected these moves and the clumsy use of the polo stick was enough to confuse the pony which had been accustomed to professional signals, obeying them immediately. The slightest variation made him jib and shy.

Of course the lad fell off and hurt himself and when the trainer came to see him in hospital there was no advice to give except that experience comes with practice and perfection is not quick to achieve. The young man never forgot that first lesson and went on to become one of the finest polo players of today.

Perhaps polo proved to him that being the top member of a gymkhana team was not enough. There was a finesse needed in handling a stick and clumsy strokes, even on a well schooled pony, could make the animal's sensitivity turn to suspicion.

One has to compare gymkhana with polo because both are active and competitive, unlike dressage or even show jumping – unless the jumping is a group event where six jumpers compete at the same time and the rider who jumps the most obstacles in a set period is the winner.

This game is compelling to watch mainly because of its thrilling anticipation for accidents.

The word polo is derived from the Tibetan *pulu,* which means a ball made from knotted willow wood – and this is always the wood used to make the balls even today.

14 HORSES IN ART

MANY artists have tried to portray the beauty of the horse. The Greeks depicted horses as far back as 940 BC and there is a cave painting in France dating from 10,000 years BC.

Portraits of famous people on their horses used to show the animals with necks too long and limbs functioning in impossible paces. The gallop was shown with front and hind legs stretched out straight and the trot as a lateral movement. But George Stubbs changed all that. He made a study of the horse's anatomy and helped to unite accuracy with artistic ability.

The earliest representations of horse drawn chariots are in Assyrian palaces. They are in bas relief and show scenes of victory in war. Horses at that time were too small to carry warriors into battle and it was not until the first millennium that larger horses were bred and, together with camels, formed the prototype of the modern cavalry.

During the classical Greek era sculpture was brought to a point of perfection and physical splendour which has never since been equalled. The horses on the frieze of the Parthenon, the temple to Athena on the Acroplis executed under the direction of Phidias, are realistic three-dimensional portrayals of these animals.

In the days of the Roman Empire the traditions of the Greeks were maintained and in some instances re-invigorated – only to be totally submerged in the dark ages which followed the collapse of Roman rule.

Equestrian art took a different form in the Far East. The Chinese horses of the T'ang period are fascinating for they all have straight front legs and cow hocks behind. Naturalism was brought back to Western art by Albrecht Durer. In his magnificent painting inspired by the Book of Revelations (vi, 2–8) the Four Horsemen of the Apocalyse are on animals that are accurately delineated in shape and movement.

In Sussex today there are many notable horse artists, the best known being Frank Wootton and Clifford and Wendy Meadway – the latter a horse portrait painter with a portfolio of more than 100 examples.

In Wilmington church there is a painting on canvas, by an unknown artist, showing farm horses at work. It was discovered in a cupboard in the village hall some years ago and was restored and placed in the church.

This seven foot high painting on linen of horses in the movements of High School is by the author. It was one of a number of his works shown at an exhibition in Brighton.

15 HORSES IN FILMS

HORSES are not specially bred for film work but they are chosen for their suitability for the sport or the period that is to be represented. Once they have been successful in a film they will always be in demand.

Just such a horse was Jackdaw, an Irish/thoroughbred cross. He appeared in so many top productions he became quite a celebrity.

Errol Flynn and Robert Taylor were among the famous stars that rode him and when he was sold by the Metro-Goldwyn-Mayer Studios at auction the previous owner was advised to buy him back as the studios would always hire him.

This they did and he was then ridden by Stanley Baker in *Knights of the Round Table* and by Stewart Granger in *The Life and Times of Beau Brummell*. Later he was used by Sir Laurence Olivier in *Richard III* and by Jean Seberg in *Saint Joan*.

Sadly he was galloped about on other films and finally broke his wind and the owner, having had the horse for a long time, both as a successful film horse and as a hunter in East Sussex, insisted that he should be retired.

Jeannette Sterk with Polly during the filming of Moonraker

In *Moonraker,* a swashbuckling adventure starring George Baker as a highwayman and set in the days

49

Eartha Kitt and her daughter rehearsing a scene for a film on Frolic and Merrylegs.

of the English Civil War, the film director asked the riders to gallop round Studland Bill. A new horse, not used to the work, got over excited and pulled ahead of the others and they followed him onto the cliff edge from which there was a sheer drop to the sea. Two or three animals lost their footing, nearly tumbling to certain death below. The horse which caused the trouble was immediately taken off the picture.

Something similar happened in *The Charge of the Light Brigade* which starred David Hemmings and Corin Redgrave. The scene had to be rehearsed and at least four of the horses got dangerously unmanageable during the takes. Eventually the assistants and the stable manager sorted out the troublemakers until the battle scenes looked realistic, not like a lot of stunt riders out of control.

Apart from film work the horses and ponies are used in other theatrical enterprises. Every year two ponies called Magic and Merrylegs had to pull Cinderella's coach in pantomime. On one engagement they were driven on stage by Hughie Green as Buttons – not very successfully as they nearly knocked the scenery over and ended up facing each other on the edge of the orchestra pit.

On another occasion two other pantomime ponies, called Mystic and Muffin, joined Merry and Magic on stage to celebrate Mystic's twenty first birthday. All the cast enjoyed the party but the stage manager was not very happy with the state of the stage when he had to prepare it for the evening performance.

For the programme *Talking Animals* the television company asked for one white horse to come galloping out of a forest. When the scene was shot and the zoo vet, David Taylor said the line: 'And then the horses came out of the forest onto the plains' not one white horse but six came dashing from the stable nearby, scattering the camera crew in their enthusiasm to illustrate the point that their tree browsing ancestors had started eating grass.

In another programme, *Animal Country,* it was proved to Desmond Morris that horse working within their herd could be ridden without bridles and bits, just on pieces of hay string. As they are herd animals they relate to each other in all circumstances and these horses gave a full Activity Performance, halting, changing the rein, cantering on given leg and passing each other in opposite directions – all without bits in their mouths. In fact the riders said they got a better reaction on just the pieces of string.

In Ireland around the twelfth century it was discovered by an invading army that Irish warriors always went into battle, not only without armour, but with just rope halters on their horses instead of bits and bridles. It was thought that the main reason for this was because their horses lived on grass and could feed whenever they wanted.

Ireland owes its reputation for horses with good bone and of high quality to its climate, which is warm and moist in winter making the grass continue to grow and contain vitamins all the year round. The subsoil is limestone which builds good bone and there is a strata of it stretching across the central plain of Ireland.

Jasmine Dee on stage in Cinderella *with Mystic and Merrylegs.*

16 THREE DAY EVENTING

ONE of the most successful venues for both three day and one day eventing is Ardingly in Sussex – and more recently Crockstead. It is a demanding but rewarding sport and needs places that cater for all three stages adequately.

Sussex produces some good riders and horses for the three different types of riding involved – dressage, cross country, and show jumping. A young person's sport you might think, but over the years there have been many mature army officers who have produced first class eventers, all schooled and bred by themselves and constant winners every time.

Eventing began as part of cavalry training in the British Army. Members of the mounted regiments were all encouraged to train their horses in these separate fields of horsemanship.

France, Belgium, Sweden and Switzerland held military three day events in the early part of the twentieth century but it was not until 1912 such competitions were included in the Olympic Games and it was after the Second World War that eventing spread to civilian life too.

The ideal horse for eventing has a good temperament because to do well in different but demanding exercises he must remain calm at all times. Whether it is a one day, two day or a three day event the training is basically the same.

There is a story that shows how training, even in impossible circumstances, can produce a first class event horse.

This is how it goes:

The owner of the sow's ear of a horse from which a silk purse was produced was an arthritic woman of sixty years. She had ridden all her life and had acquired a 16 hh bay gelding from a gypsy who had tethered it on the verge near her home.

It was poor but, apart from needing food, it had the right tempera ment for intelligent schooling. Perhaps she recognised this and felt she had the knowledge to create a high class event horse from this poor creature. This is exactly what she did.

She lived in an end-of-terrace house in suburbia, her only facility a cowshed and a small paddock. The cowshed became a stable with thick straw bedding and bulging haynets night and morning, and when the horse improved in condition she started riding him. Fortunately it was in the spring so she had the summer ahead and her little paddock proved a dry, springy place in which to school him.

She had to have help mounting the horse, because of her arthritis, but when she was in the saddle the animal came to life. Apparently she had ridden in Austria and had been taught the classical movements of dressage and this proved the best form of riding to get the horse fit. The show jumping came a lot later and the cross country later still but the dressage improved and prepared him for what was to come.

The woman knew she could only take him so far but she had a show-jumping nephew and when the time came her nephew was summoned for the job.

He was kept under strict control by his aunt and not allowed to escape the training programme. To give him his due, he became as keen as she to prepare the gelding for his future role. An army trainer who had known the woman's ex-husband happened to hear of what she was doing and came along to applaud. He was so impressed by what he saw that he arranged for the horse to continue training in his own yard under very professional guidance.

The result was one of the finest eventers during the early years of the sport's popularity and both the elderly owner and her nephew loved every minute of it.

The training of the eventer is a good all round training and getting a horse fit for the job is an art in itself. At one time the horse's main importance was in agriculture and as a vehicle for man to get easily from one point to another across country. Nowadays the horse is used most of the time for pleasure and, of course, competition. In this capacity the animal must be trained and knowledge used to get him in proper condition.

It can be an interesting science and no doubt has improved from

Taking a jump on the cross country course.

those early days. It is a pity some people still believe that a horse or pony is 'living naturally' in a small paddock and needs nothing more than the grass at its feet. In a natural setting the moorland or the forest ponies can range far and wide and are not limited to one small, fenced paddock.

First the conditions, then the training. Any sphere of equestrianism must be carefully planned and have an accepted way of progression. No Western style breaking his spirit, like the cowboys who, in some parts of the world tie the animal securely to a post and wait for him to become exhausted before putting on a saddle and bridle, mounting and pushing the horse into a gallop until he is exhausted even more. It is then said that the animal has been 'broken-in' within three days.

In fact it is easy handling that wins in the end and a gentle approach that gives a horse confidence to trust, not to fear, his trainer.

There is a right type for every job and an eventer is no exception. He must be tough for the cross country section, yet calm and obedient in the dressage and free moving in the show jumping. A five or six year old thoroughbred or three quarter bred is ideal.

Trekking without hats in 1965 and (below) trekking with hats in 1995

17 TREKKING

ACCORDING to the dictionary trekking means undertaking a long arduous journey, but sitting on a pony for hours on end is surely only arduous for the pony? Or is it?

After six hours trekking in the mountains of Scotland, even with lunch breaks in between, riders who have never sat on a pony before are crippled with aches and pains. Actually the higher paths are easier to hack over because they are drained and springy and on good treks the animals are led up steep craggy paths by their riders. It is the moorland treks that can be boggy and difficult to ride over.

In any case a lot of people have had their first taste of riding by going on a trek. Reliable trekking centres usually have good safe native-bred ponies and as they have lived in a herd they follow each other naturally. This helps the trek leaders who work in pairs when the trek is a large one, one taking the lead position and the other the rear.

It is the one in the rear who has the worst job. He has to teach the riders how to use their legs and hands so that the string can keep safely together. If the riders learn how to post in the trot all well and good but unless they are trekking every day for say a week, they have to sit or bump most of the trotting time.

Usually the pace is kept to a walk but occasionally, in order to keep the string together, it is necessary to make some of the animals amble into a trot. It is surprising how youngsters, if they trek for a whole week, develop a rising trot and quite a bit of independence in the seat. Going straight, as opposed to riding in circles, does help the seat which forms the basis of all riding. It does not, however, help the pony and often trekking ponies are very one-sided in their paces.

The aim is to explore the countryside and long, slow hacks through lovely scenery, with sometimes views of the sea, are most enjoyable. In Canada there are more ambitious trail-riding holidays on horseback and in America there are camps, particularly for children, where they teach both Western and European styles of riding.

Once a new pony trekking centre opened near a lengthy stretch of open beach. Everything was newly acquired – saddles and bridles, open horse lines with hay racks and pillar reins so that the animals could be tacked up and attached to the posts ready for the riders. The trouble was that the whole thing had been set up on the top of a cliff – and it was always windy.

However, the opening day was great success and a full house booked in for a whole week. The local press came to photograph the first pony trek from the new premises and all the riders were carefully mounted with stirrups just right and neck straps to steady their hands. The string looked elegant as it wended its way through the Downland towards the open beach.

The little moorland ponies had never seen a beach before and as they approached it they looked much livelier than when they started out.

The trek leaders did not stand a chance. It only took one pony to squeal with delight and kick up its hindlegs for the whole lot to get the message – and they were off like a shot from a gun.

The riders were taken quite by surprise and with their total lack of equestrian ability screamed in terror as they galloped madly towards the sea. There were no hedges or paths to fence them in and the trek leaders could only make matters worse by charging after them.

Most of the trekkers fell off in the water but some stayed on long enough to reach a nice grassy slope where their ponies decided to have a lovely meal. As they then bent down the screaming riders were catapulted over their heads.

This all took place at one of the earlier trekking centres and nowadays such incidents are most unlikely to occur. Today's trek leaders avoid great stretches of open beach and use sensible tracks and field edges so they can maintain control.

On that disastrous trek there were twenty ponies but today treks are limited to a much smaller number. Five of the riders on that first venture lost their nerve and never got on a horse again. The others, when some order was regained, carried on and have since been able to laugh about the incident and become regular yearly trekkers.

People who have always wanted to ride horses but never had the opportunity in their youth can get pleasure out of trekking in their later years. Even riding in all weathers does not daunt the enthusiast and tack shops have stocked up with some of the best clothes for the sport. Mind you, riding in very wet and cold conditions can dampen the townee who has visions of lovely grassy tracks, sunshine and the company of others equally devoted to horses.

Often the riders come home frozen stiff, however well wrapped up they are. The grassy tracks have been sodden with rain, the ditches overflowing, the sun covered with a drenching cloud and the other riders not animal minded in the sentimental sense.

Trekkers should always be encouraged to handle their animal, to pick out the feet, to groom off the mud, learn how to tack up and listen to the advise of their trek leaders.

18 DRESSAGE

DRESSAGE is high precision riding. It is not necessarily a spectator sport, like show jumping, but it is of great interest to those who like to see horses well trained, performing routines with balance and cadence.

Flying changes in canter, the high trot of *passage* and *piaffer*, and making movements precisely from given marks in the riding arena may bore some people as one rider after another does the same test but there are always different tests to watch.

The art of dressage is increasing as more and more people are waking up to the joy of establishing a partnership with their horses when they teach them grace and suppleness in movement.

Perhaps driving dressage is more a spectator sport, for after all it has many more difficulties. It consists of eleven movements and assessments of general impression. It can be done in single, double, tandem or four-in-hand turn outs. There is no lateral work and circles are not less than twenty metres in diameter. There are also fewer pace variations. There is the ordinary walk, the working, collected and extended trots and the rein-back but their relative simplicity only slightly compensates for the difficulty of getting a four-in-hand moving with precision.

In ridden dressage the tests are:

PRELIMINARY which includes basic paces, circles in trot and canter, progressive transitions, and even trot to a halt.

NOVICE in which the circles are smaller and there is the serpentine and lengthening of the stride.

ELEMENTARY which includes even smaller circles and simple changes at canter, also some lateral collection.

ADVANCED ELEMENTARY starts to look more interesting with shoulder-in and canters down to ten metres.

This drawing by Wendy Meadway shows the moment of suspension in the canter.

In **MEDIUM** the circles are down to eight metres, there is counter-cantering round the arena, and at the end the half pass, the rein-back and half *pirouettes* at a walk.

MEDIUM ADVANCED has even smaller circles, an even half pass at the canter and single flying changes.

ADVANCED gets more exciting with zigzags at half pass, canter in the serpentine and half *pirouettes* at the canter. Also there is now four time flying changes and transitions from canter to halt.

The **PRIX ST GEORGE** includes the **Intermediate 1** and **2** with canter zigzags at half pass with flying changes, and flying changes every four strides. Finally there is the

GRAND PRIX ST GEORGE when the *piaffer* and *passage* is introduced and still to come is the

GRAND PRIX ST GEORGE SPECIAL in which one of the most difficult movements must be the *pirouette* at the canter.

The competitive markings give up to ten points for every movement, coming down a point progressively from very good to very bad and a nought if the movement is not performed.

The dressage rule book runs to seventy one pages and there are more than 500 judges listed. Among the great number of rules the horse grinding its teeth or swishing its tail can lose points as these are taken as signs of resistance. The rider is prohibited from using his or her voice and an error in the sequence of movements incurs penalty marks and, after the fourth error, elimination.

A local young woman who not only bred her own horses for dressage but schooled them herself is an example of the dedication and determination this form of equestrian artistry seems to foster.

After a number of years her hard work and constant practice paid off and she has now got one of her horses into **PRIX ST GEORGE** competition, which means she has to wear a top hat and tail coat.

Her trainer insisted that she stretch herself and take the test although she thought she was not ready.

All the required movements are now coming along well and she is gaining points at every meeting. At her first attempt, to come twenty fifth out of fifty entries was an achievement. The standard is always high and at every event now she is gaining places.

She was eliminated once for carrying a stick which she knew was not allowed in that test but it happened inadvertently. As she entered the arena a steward, who should have known better, told her she had forgotten her stick and gave her one. She was too nervous to refuse it.

On several occasions a woman with a weight problem did very well in most competitions but the spectators rather unkindly enjoyed a laugh

This group of horses performed a dressage competition without bridles on the television programme Animal Country.

at her expense when she invariably lost the rhythm of the extended trot and could not help wobbling like a jelly across the diagonal line.

Horses under strict control do not drop or urinate but it does happen sometimes and always at the wrong moment. One immaculate horseman came down the centre line, gave a perfect halt, saluted – and his horse straddled and urinated with much splashing.

It is difficult to discipline an animal but any human member of a dressage group participating at a dressage competition who behaves in a disgraceful manner or in a way that may bring the name of the group into disrepute is considered to be in breach of the rules.

Punishment could be a reprimand, disqualification, suspension, expulsion or a fine which must be paid before the offending rider is allowed to compete again.

19 HIGH SCHOOL

HIGH School is non-competitive dressage and includes movements that are taken from a book written in 400 BC by the Athenian writer, Xenophon. Unfortunately the progression of this classical riding, due to wars, was lost for nearly 2,000 years but the precepts of Xenophon which were, in fact, based on even earlier authority, Simon of Athens, are adhered to today by all great riding masters.

It was on them that the renaissance of classical riding was based in the seventeenth century. At the time another great teacher, Frederico Grisone, created High School equitation, but he differed from Xenophon's complete understanding and kindness in training, by his insistence on greater use of force.

One of his pupils became the Court Riding Master to Louis XIII and another, Pignatelli, the *Ecuyer* of the famous riding academy in Naples.

Pignatelli methods were based more on Xenophon's and advocated more humane methods of training. There was a keenness throughout Europe for a great revival of High School riding and some magnificent riding halls were built in which to practice it. The most famous of all was the Spanish Riding School in Vienna which held top place for its superb demonstrations of *haute école*.

With the French Revolution a lot were destroyed but fortunately the one in Vienna has survived to this day.

Up to the outbreak of the First World War the Spanish Riding School was supreme in the art of riding and even after the Second World War it was the Spanish School of Vienna, with its famous Lipizzaner horses, that completely dominated the classical scene.

High School riding was introduced into Britain in the 1930s. It is practised in America where there is even a Lippizaner stud that sends out teams of riders who perform the airs and the movements at exhibition in Europe.

To train a horse to **GRAND PRIX** dressage demands the skill of

The High School movement, the Spanish Walk, performed by the author's Lipizzaner stallion, Henry.

haute-ecole and includes such movements as the *pirouette, passage* and *piaffer*, but horses can be trained even further.

In Vienna they are trained to do the famous Airs Above the Ground – the *passade, levade, courbette, croupade*, and *capriole*. Most of these exercises are off-ground or partly off-ground when either the forelegs or hindlegs are raised. They are theatrical enough for circus riders to copy and one often sees them performing a *levade* and possibly a *courbette*. The former is a stationary rear and the latter the horse performs small jumps forward on his hind legs.

The name Spanish for the school dates from 1580 when horses were brought from the Iberian Peninsula, which was part of the empire of the Spanish Habsburgs, to Lipizza, a province among the crown lands of the Austrian branch of the family.

Vera Cody McLeod on her Palomino Goldie, performing on stage.

In 1580 Lipizza was considered an Imperial Stud with the best horses and it supplied to the court stables in Vienna. Additional Spanish horses were bought regularly during the eighteenth century and they were to sire prosperous lines, in fact their direct descendants can still be seen performing in the Spanish Riding School today. As a result of the 1939–45 War the stud is now at Piber.

There is a tale to tell about a Sussex horsewoman who spent her whole life training horses in High School. She had several horses but only three showed the exceptional signs needed for *haute-école*.

Her first one, known as Bracken, was part thoroughbred and the second, a Palomino named Goldie, was used by Max Bygraves as part of his variety act. Her third horse was a brown and white Irish cob – Sorrel. All three were ridden by their owner in the circus and on the variety stage. Her stage name was Vera Cody and she was married to Tex McLeod, the cowboy film star.

To see Vera give a performance anywhere – in a field, a manège, or on stage – was something to be remembered. She not only rode her horses in High School, using all the movements, but also got the horse to perform them in harness. Vera was once shown on television sitting in the trap giving hand and voice signals only.

The author owned a Lipizzaner stallion named Henry which he used for exhibition – performing most movements including the Airs Above the Ground. He often rode the animal into dance halls where he led the dancing and performed the *passage, piaffe* and *pirouette* with the horse wearing special rubber shoes.

The horse had been given to the Nepalese Ambassador as a diplomatic present but as the recipient did not ride the author bought him through a diplomatic connection and with the help of Vera learned the aids needed to ride this special horse. Like most of the Lipizzaners Henry was white/grey in colour. As this colour is dominant in the breed they are chosen for exhibition in Vienna.

Whatever else has collapsed the Spanish Riding School is still the only surviving school of horsemanship in the world and the institution cannot help but receive the recognition it deserves. Let us hope it survives for posterity and in years to come the world will offer its gratitude – after all, it did start 400 years BC.

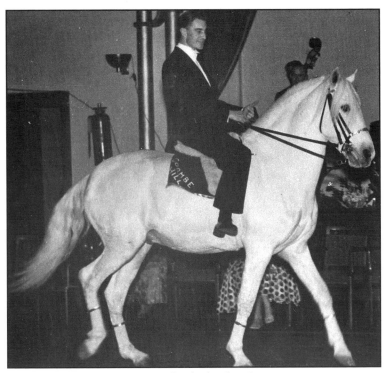

Henry leads the dancing

Put a herd of fresh horses into a field and you will immediately see the glimmerings of *haute-école* but put them into a field full of jumps and they will ignore them.

This does not mean horses cannot jump as proved by a local show-jumping horse who always jumped his field gate or his stable door at feeding time. He had a natural ability, which was encouraged by his owner, but he would still ignore the practice jumps when turned out into his paddock.

This surely proves the point that the most natural athletics for a horse must be High School. They only jump when the incentive is irresistible, or created artificially as in the Airs Above the Ground. It is fortunate that horses are trainable and respond to every level of schooling, but their inbred ability must be discovered first.

Humans and animals have their limitations. One man can become a mathematician and another a composer of music, both are intelligent and sensitive and we must accept that animals have a similar pattern. In all stories of equine success lies the discovery of an animal's natural ability and their response to a particular trainer. When the two come together there is always the recognition of genius.

Vera Cody schooled three horses to High School, and she always said that her greatest success was in Sorrel but she had the greatest love for her first horse, Bracken.

This is understandable. Sometimes the horse who trains well is too much an individual to love but the difficult one who suffers failure before success is always lovable. It is the closeness built up for all animals working with their trainers every day that develops respect and understanding. Small signs from both are immediately interpreted and actually looked for in every phase of the programme.

Man's unity with the horse is sacrosanct.

20 A CAROL SERVICE
FOR HORSES

FOR many years a stable in Sussex has held a carol service for horses. It was started in a London stable but when the horses came down to their new home in the country the event came with them and has been a much loved Christmas party ever since.

It takes place in an indoor school which has a large lighted tree reaching forty feet up into the rafters. Coloured jump poles are used as divisions in which the horses stand during the service, but before this they are brought to the tree to receive gifts of sliced apples and carrots.

Their leaders usually groom them thoroughly and decorate their head collars in tinsel and ribbon. The vicar kindly comes and takes the service and there is a collection for animal charities, which always reaches a three figure total.

Afterwards health is drunk in coffee and the horses finish off the rest of their presents. One local resident always brings neatly wrapped gifts of oatcakes and mints for each one of the animals. After so long the older horses know the routine and their leaders can barely stop them rushing up to the tree when their turn comes.

One old mare has to be brought in by bridle as she cannot be controlled in a head collar. Even when she is peacefully standing in her place she cannot resist the sight of all the presents and has been known to charge forward during the service nearly knocking the vicar to his knees.

A horse new to the service thought all the presents were meant for him and during a quiet prayer took his leader back to the tree several times for more. It was part of the fun and everyone including the animals loved every minute. One local says it is a part of Christmas that means the festive season has really started and he cannot now visualise being without it.

Horses coming to the tree for their presents at the annual carol service in a stable at Wilmington.

The weather is often wet and windy but one memorable time we had a lovely stillness with a layer of snow everywhere – not a blizzard, just that magical night when all is white and the trees dusted with frost. Of course there had to be a moon and in one corner of the old stable yard, a crib.

Perhaps this was the picture, and others like it, that gave people the real feeling of Christmas when they came to the carol service and the horse's tree. After all – Jesus was born in a stable.

ABOUT THE AUTHOR

KENNETH QUICKE has been with horses all his life, having lived in the country and had ponies from an early age. In his late teens he became a Redcoat and was riding instructor for Billy Butlin, but decided one season was enough.

He and his wife Patricia started the Coombe Hill Stables at Kingston upon Thames in 1948. It was from here that he did ten years as a stunt rider in films, sometimes using his Lipizzaner stallion, Henry, and doubling for stars of the day.

He retired to the East Sussex village of Wilmington with a team of grey horses and there he teaches riding locally and has students in the summer.

Kenneth has had his horses on television, once with Desmond Morris and Sarah Kennedy in *Animal Country* and with David Taylor in *Talking Animal*. When David asked for one white horse to gallop into a field, Kenneth gave him ten – and they were used in the title shots throughout the series.

French students at the Wilmington Equestrian Centre – on nine of Kenneth's ten grey horses.